Black Things

By Sally Cowan

Lots of things are black.

This is my black cat, Bliss.

Bliss sits on the steps
in the sun.

Bliss

Bam!

Bliss is quick.

She can get a bug!

bug

I have a black fish, too!

This is Chuck.

Chuck

Dad's big dog is Dash.

Dash has long legs
and lots of black blobs.

black blobs

Mum has black chickens
in a big black pen.

This hen is Bling.

She has black feathers.

When Bling had chicks,
some were black.

Bling

black chicks

This is the bub, Cash.

Cash plays with blocks.
Some blocks have black
on them.

blocks

I like black things!

CHECKING FOR MEANING

1. Where does Bliss, the black cat, like to sit? *(Literal)*

2. What does Dash have that is black? *(Literal)*

3. What could Cash do with the blocks? *(Inferential)*

EXTENDING VOCABULARY

black	What are other things you know that are black? E.g. the night sky, liquorice, clothes.
blobs	What are *blobs*? What is another word that has a similar meaning? Use this word in the sentence, *Dash has black* ____.
blocks	Look at the word *blocks*. What is the base of this word? How has adding *s* changed the meaning of the word? Find another word in the book where *s* has been added to make it mean more than one.

MOVING BEYOND THE TEXT

1. What things do you have that are black?

2. Are the black things in this book always black or can they be other colours?

3. If you wrote a book called *Red Things*, what would you include in it?

4. What is your favourite colour? Why?

SPEED SOUNDS

| bl | gl | cr | fr | st |

PRACTICE WORDS

Bliss

black

steps

Bling

blobs

blocks